THE CHANGING FACE OF
GERMANY

Text by SONJA SCHANZ
Photographs by BOB SMITH

RAINTREE
STECK-VAUGHN
RSVP ® PUBLISHERS

A Harcourt Company

Austin   New York
www.raintreesteckvaughn.com

Published by Raintree Steck-Vaughn Publishers, an imprint of Steck-Vaughn Company

Library of Congress Cataloging-in-Publication Data is available upon request

ISBN 0-7398-5489-5

Printed in Italy. Bound in the United States.

1 2 3 4 5 6 7 8 9 0 LB 07 06 05 04 03 02

Acknowledgments

The publishers would like to thank the following for their contributions to this book: Rob Bowden—statistics research; Peter Bull—map illustration; Nick Hawken—statistics panel illustrations. All photographs are by Bob Smith except page 6 (Popperfoto). Note: figures given in statistics panels for the period before unification represent the average of the combined figures for East and West Germany.

Contents

Berlin—A New Era

When the Berlin Wall came down on November 9, 1989, it marked the beginning of a new era for Berlin. Since 1949, Berlin and Germany had been divided (you can find out more about this on page 6). East Berlin was the capital of the eastern part of Germany, the German Democratic Republic (GDR). West Berlin was part of the Federal Republic of Germany, but it was completely surrounded by the GDR. In 1961, the government of the GDR built a huge wall across the city to separate east and west.

In the late 1980s, political changes took place across eastern Europe. The Berlin Wall was torn down. Germany became one country again, with Berlin as its capital. The city faced major challenges. It had to combine into one system all the different systems that had been used to run the city when it was divided. A vast building program was also needed, to house the government of a united Germany and to provide all the facilities required by a modern European capital.

The Potsdamer Platz is an example of the changes that are taking place. Until 1990 it was a vast, empty space in the middle of the divided city. When all the building projects are completed, there will be a huge shopping mall, movie theaters, musical theaters, a casino, and also the German and European headquarters of many of the world's largest corporations. The Potsdamer Platz will be at the heart of Berlin.

▲ *Modern buildings in Berlin's Potsdamer Platz.*

◄ *People enjoy strolling along the Unter den Linden, under the lime trees that give this famous street its name.*

NORTH SEA

Baltic Sea

Husum

SCHLESWIG-
HOLSTEIN

MECKLENBURG-
WESTERN
POMERANIA

HAMBURG
Hamburg

BREMEN
Bremen

Elbe

LOWER
SAXONY

Weser

Ems

Hanover

Oder

BERLIN
Berlin

POLAND

NETHERLANDS

Rhine

SAXONY-
ANHALT

BRANDENBURG

HARZ
MTS

Cottbus

NORTH RHINE-
WESTPHALIA

Elbe

Halle

Cologne

THURINGIA

Leipzig

BELGIUM

Bonn

G E R M A N Y

SAXONY

HESSE

RHINELAND-
PALATINATE

Frankfurt am Main

Main

CZECH
REPUBLIC

LUXEMBOURG

Moselle

Rhine

Main

SAARLAND

Mannheim

0   100   200   300 km

Stuttgart

Danube

BAVARIA

FRANCE

Neckar

BADEN

BLACK FOREST

WURTTEMBURG

Munich

Freiburg

Chiemsee

Lake
Constance

A L P S

SWITZERLAND

Zugspitze

AUSTRIA

N

▲ *This map shows Germany's major cities and landscape features, as well as places mentioned in this book.*

GERMANY: KEY FACTS

Area: 137,738 square miles (356,733 square km)

Population: 81,896,000 (1996 census)

Population density: 594 people per square mile (229 people per square km)

Capital: Berlin (3,459,000)

Other main cities: Hamburg (1,700,000); Munich (1,200,000); Cologne (964,000);
Frankfurt am Main (648,000)

Highest mountain: Zugspitze 9,721 feet (2,963 m)

Longest river: Rhine 537 miles (865 km)

Main language: German and its many dialects

Major religions: 27.6 million Protestants; 27.5 million Roman Catholics; 2.6 million Muslims;
70,000 Jews

Currency: Euro

Sources: *Facts about Germany* (German Government Information Service); *Deutschland nach der Wende*
(Verlag für Deutsch, 1999/2000)

2 Past Times

Following its defeat in World War II (1939–1945), Germany was divided and occupied by the four Allies—the United States, Britain, France, and the Soviet Union. After some disagreement between the Allies, two separate German states were founded in 1949. The Federal Republic of Germany (FDR, also known as West Germany), with Bonn as its capital, was set up under the influence of the United States, Britain, and France. Its political and economic systems were similar to theirs. The German Democratic Republic (GDR, also known as East Germany), with East Berlin as its capital, was founded under the influence of the Soviet Union. Like the Soviet Union, it was run as a communist state.

Life was very different for the people of the two German states. In West Germany they enjoyed political freedom and a high standard of living. Life was tougher in East Germany. There was no political freedom, no freedom to travel, and a shortage of consumer goods. On the positive side, there was no unemployment and both women and men played a vital role in the economy.

▼ The building of the Berlin Wall in 1961. It separated East and West Berlin for 28 years.

Germany Reunited

In the late 1980s, there were big political changes in the Soviet Union. Eventually, communist governments throughout Europe collapsed—including the government of East Germany. As a result, Germany was reunited in 1990. The new Germany is made up of sixteen federal states, based on the system used in the former West Germany. Each of the federal states has its own government, with some freedom to decide its own policies on issues such as education.

Germany and the European Union

West Germany was one of the six countries that set up the European Economic Community (EEC) in 1957. The EEC has now expanded to become the European Union, and the reunited Germany is one of its strongest supporters. Germany was one of the countries that abolished its national currency, the Deutschmark, in favor of the European currency, the euro, in 2002.

▲ *The Reichstag, the German parliament building in Berlin. After unification, a glass dome was added to the old building, allowing people to look down into the chamber.*

IN THEIR OWN WORDS

"I am Heide Drost and I lived in East Germany until unification in October 1990. The organization I was working for closed down because there was an organization doing the same work in the west. I got a job in the tourist industry, but the firm failed after one year. My next job was with an airline, but unfortunately this company also closed within one year. I decided to start my own travel agency. It flourished and so I stayed in work until I retired in 2001. The process of unification was hard and painful for many people, including myself, but I don't want to turn the clock back, and I have a good life now."

3

Landscape and Climate

Germany lies at the very heart of Europe. No other European nation shares borders with as many countries as Germany. Its nine neighbors are Denmark in the north, the Netherlands, Belgium, Luxembourg, and France in the west, Switzerland and Austria in the south, and the Czech Republic and Poland in the east. Germany is also the largest country in Europe, in terms of both area and population.

Coasts and Plains

Northern Germany lies low and flat, with wide plains and open valleys. Large cornfields, green meadows with grazing cattle and sheep, and solitary farmhouses surrounded by clumps of trees are typical of the area. Woods, forests, heathland, and some small hills are found only in the eastern parts of the region, in an area called Holsteinische Schweiz.

There is marshland along the North Sea coast and around the islands. Here, houses and farms are built on mounds that have been created to protect them from storm tides and floods. The Baltic Sea coast is notable for its white, chalky cliffs, which contrast spectacularly with the expanse of flat, sandy beach below them.

Northern Germany also includes major areas of population and industry, such as the industrial region of North Rhine-Westphalia in the west, Greater Berlin, and the cities of Hamburg, Bremen, Halle, and Leipzig.

▲ *The Luneburg Heath, north of Hanover, is the largest heathland in Germany.*

◀ *Beach baskets are a typical feature of both the North and Baltic Sea coasts. They protect people from too much sun or too much wind.*

IN THEIR OWN WORDS

"My name is Silvelin Schröter. I work for BUND, the German Friends of the Earth. This picture shows me (standing) with some of my colleagues. Protecting Germany's natural environment is very important to us. We have to be consulted before any major building plans can be carried out. If we think the environmental impact will be too serious, we try to have the plan stopped or altered.

"One of our main areas of work is information and communication. We produce a monthly magazine for our members, as well as information packs and other publications. We also fund research and publish the results.

"Through our campaigning and publicity, we have played an important part in getting certain pesticides banned. We support organic farming and its products, campaign to improve the quality of water in rivers, and promote alternatives to the car as a means of transportation. We are an important organization in Germany and have achieved a lot since we were founded 20 years ago."

Hills, Mountains, and Rivers

To the south of the city of Hanover, the countryside changes. Rolling hills and mountains, largely covered with woods and forests, stretch south to the River Danube. Between the forested areas, there are meadows and fields where a variety of crops are grown.

In the far south, a small strip of the Alps, about 150 miles (240 km) long, falls within Germany's borders and includes the country's highest mountain, the Zugspitze, 9,721 feet (2,963 m).

Small, picturesque villages are located in the long, and often deep, river valleys. This is the scenery most often associated with Germany. However, towns, major cities, and a wide range of industries, including car factories, chemical plants, and textile factories, are situated in the river valleys too.

The River Rhine, flowing from Lake Constance to the North Sea, is an important route for tourist boats and cargo barges traveling between north and south. Many major cities and towns are located along the Rhine. The Rhine valley is also well known for wine growing and for its many castles. Like the other wine-growing areas around the Moselle and Main rivers, it has become an important tourist attraction.

▲ The Rhine, at 537 miles (865 km), is the longest and most important river in Germany.

Climate and Climate Change

Germany's climate is moderate, but temperatures in both summer and winter can vary greatly. In summer, the temperature may be anywhere between 64 and 95 °F (18 and 35 °C). In winter, there can be a lot of snow, with temperatures as low as -5 (20 °C), or it can be mild and never colder than 39 to 41 °F (3 to

IN THEIR OWN WORDS

"I am Regine Schmidt and I am a geography teacher. I have lived in southern Germany for 12 years. I like the warm summers here, and even winters are not too cold, with an average temperature of about 32 °F (0 °C).

"Climate changes, in particular warmer temperatures, have been observed all over the world. I think we have warmer winters with less snow here in southern Germany than we did when I was a child. In 1999, there was also an unusually severe storm here causing a lot of damage, which some scientists attribute to climate changes. But who knows for sure?"

5 °C). The coldest areas are the high mountains, and the warmest are the Rhine, Neckar, Main, and Moselle valleys.

What change global warming will bring is not yet clear. Many Germans, however, are quick to blame unusually cool summers, mild winters, or heavy rainfall on a change in the climate.

▼ *A cable car takes people to the top of the mountain called Schauinsland near Freiburg in the Black Forest.*

4

Natural Resources

Minerals and Energy Reserves

The main energy sources used in Germany are oil, gas, coal, and nuclear energy. Germany has little in the way of mineral reserves and is therefore largely dependent on imports. Two-thirds of its energy resources and considerable amounts of minerals have to be bought from other countries. Germany does, however, have large deposits of two types of coal—anthracite, a hard coal, and lignite, a softer brown coal. It also mines salt and can supply about a quarter of the natural gas it uses from its own reserves in Lower Saxony, Saxony-Anhalt, and Bavaria.

Mining for Fossil Fuels

The main hard coal deposits are found in the Saarland and in the Ruhr region of North Rhine-Westphalia, which was the center of industrial life in post-war Germany. Hard coal is expensive to mine, however, and it is being replaced as an energy source by cheaper oil, gas, or imported coal. Today, Germany's hard coal mines supply only 14 percent of the country's energy needs.

The major lignite deposits are found in the Rhineland and in southern Brandenburg, Saxony, and Saxony-Anhalt. Lignite was the main energy source in East Germany, but opencast mining for lignite had a disastrous effect on the landscape, and its uncontrolled use caused enormous environmental pollution. Lignite mining has been drastically reduced since unification, but it still remains one of Germany's main energy sources, especially for electricity generation.

▼ *Opencast lignite mining near Cottbus in the east of Germany.*

Nuclear Power

In 2002, there were 19 nuclear power plants in operation. Nuclear power is, however, very unpopular in Germany, and the government has now promised to phase out nuclear power completely by 2030.

Alternative Energy

Only five percent of Germany's energy comes from a renewable source. Most of this is from hydroelectric power plants. There are many projects that explore the efficiency of solar and wind energy. These are subsidized by national and state governments, companies, and even local communities.

▲ *Strong winds from the sea sweep across the open northern plains, where wind turbines have been set up to generate electricity.*

IN THEIR OWN WORDS

"My name is Karl-Heinz Heirich and I own a small company that installs central-heating systems. We were one of the first companies to introduce and promote solar heating systems 30 years ago. Since then, solar technology has advanced steadily and has become more efficient. I use solar heating in my office. Solar panels on the roof heat water that flows through these pipes and into the hot water cylinder. However, in Germany it is not possible to heat a public or private building with solar energy alone—we don't get enough sunshine here! It can only be used as support for central-heating systems that run on oil or gas."

Agriculture

About 50 percent of the land in Germany is used for agriculture. Although many smaller farms in the west have closed down since 1945, changes in agriculture have led to big increases in productivity.

The chief agricultural products are milk, pork, beef, cereals, potatoes, and sugar beet, and, in some regions, wine, fruit, and a variety of vegetables. However, Germans now tend to eat fewer cereals and potatoes and more meat and imported food. The subsidies paid by the European Union (EU) for many of Germany's agricultural products are being reduced. As a result of these changes, farmers are increasingly switching to cultivating fodder crops and oil plants. They are also encouraged to leave more and more farmland fallow because more food is being produced in the EU than is needed.

Organic Farming

There is a growing awareness of the environmental damage caused by the pesticides and fertilizers used in farming. There have also been many scandals surrounding the overproduction of food in the EU. This has led to an increase in organic farming in Germany. The government provides

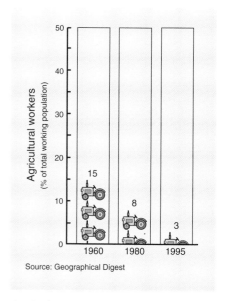

Source: Geographical Digest

▲ Only a very small percentage of German workers are now employed in agriculture.

▼ Growing grapes for wine-making is important in some regions, such as here in the Rhine valley, near Mannheim.

IN THEIR OWN WORDS

"I am Rudolf Bertram and I am responsible for 2,050 acres (830 hectares) of forest and a group of forest workers. Our job in winter is choosing and cutting down trees and selling the timber to industry. In spring we look after the young trees and plant new ones. During the summer, when a lot of people come to enjoy walking or cycling in the forests, we look after facilities such as barbecue areas, nature trails, and so on.

"Our forests are in relatively good condition now. The government made it a policy in the 1980s to preserve and restore our forests, to enlarge them where necessary, and to ensure their proper management."

financial help because it recognizes the role of farming in conserving the countryside and creating a good environment for people to live in.

Forestry

Almost a third of Germany's land is covered by forests. About two-thirds of the wood and wood products Germany needs is supplied by home-grown timber. A replanting program has ensured that more trees grow than are felled.

▼ *This once lively harbor in Husum, northern Germany, is today home to only a few shrimp-fishing boats or boats used for leisure activities.*

Fishing

Germany's principal fishing areas are the North and Baltic Seas and the Atlantic Ocean west of the United Kingdom and around Greenland. A reduction in the areas where Germany is allowed to fish combined with fewer fish in the sea have led to the decline of the German fishing industry. Today only 20 percent of the fish eaten in Germany is supplied by German fishing boats.

5

The Changing Environment

Air Pollution

The vast majority of Germans—88 percent—live in cities and towns. The biggest conurbation is the Rhine–Ruhr region, where about 11 million people live. Homes, stores, offices, and industries use large amounts of electricity, which has to be generated in power plants. There is an extensive network of highways and other roads, used by many cars and trucks. As living standards increase, people are able to buy more cars.

In the 1970s, people in Germany noticed with growing alarm that forests, which cover 30 percent of Germany's land area, were dying. The cause was air pollution, produced by power plants, industries, and exhaust fumes from vehicles.

Tackling the Problem

The sight of dying trees shocked people. Woods and forests are not only loved by German people, they are also an important natural resource for the timber industry. People demanded immediate action from the government.

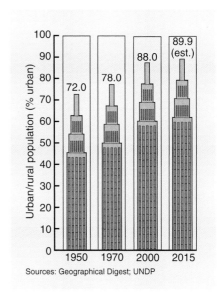

Sources: Geographical Digest; UNDP

▲ *The percentage of the population living in towns and cities has increased steadily over the last 50 years.*

◀ *Modern filter systems fitted in factories and power plants remove many polluting chemicals. Sulphur dioxide emissions have decreased by 75 percent, nitrogen oxide by 65 percent.*

A consequence of this concern was the founding of the Green Party in 1980. In 1982, the first measures for the protection of the forests were introduced. Industries had to reduce their emissions. Cars had to have catalytic converters and emission controls and had to use unleaded gas.

Air pollution has been reduced dramatically since the early 1980s. Forests have recovered due to cleaner air and a replanting program. But the problems are by no means solved. The volume of car traffic remains high. Efforts are being made to create engines that cause less damage to the environment and to improve the public transportation system, so that people will choose to leave their cars at home.

▶ *Reliable streetcar and subway systems encourage people to leave their cars at home. This streetcar carries bikes up a steep hill in Stuttgart for cyclists who are too tired to pedal!*

IN THEIR OWN WORDS

"I am Elisabeth Mayer and I work as a volunteer for CarShare in Stuttgart. CarShare is an organization that exists in every major city in Germany. In Stuttgart we have 1,400 members and 70 vehicles of various sizes. Our members choose not to have their own private car. Instead, they share a car with other members for a yearly payment. They normally walk, cycle, or use public transportation, but when they need a car for a special purpose, they book one from CarShare for as long as they need it. CarShare is an ideal solution for big cities with good public transportation systems. It does not work in rural areas, where people have to rely on their car every day."

Water Pollution

Drinking water in Germany comes mainly from rivers, lakes, and groundwater. The more polluted these are, the more difficult and expensive it becomes to produce high-quality drinking water. In the early 1970s, many rivers, such as the Rhine and the Main, were heavily polluted. There was little control over the discharge of waste water from industry, power plants, and homes. This led to a drastic decline in the diversity of fish and other creatures that lived in these rivers.

◄ *Phosphates in household laundry and cleaning products used to cause significant water pollution. Now phosphate-free products are available.*

Protection of Rivers and Lakes

In West Germany, new and tougher laws led to the construction of new sewage treatment facilities. The result was a major improvement in water quality. Fish stocks have recovered, and there are now as many different fish in the rivers as there were in 1920. Since 1990, these laws have applied to the former East Germany too. The cleanup of rivers and lakes has started, but it will be some time before they reach the standard of the rivers and lakes in the former West Germany.

The biggest water pollutants today come from farming. Artificial fertilizers and pesticides are washed off the fields by rain and into streams, rivers, and lakes. The promotion of organic farming is seen as one way of controlling this problem.

IN THEIR OWN WORDS

"My name is Rolf Pfeiffer. I work at a big sewage plant that cleans the waste water used by 600,000 people. We also clean up waste water from industries.

"The water in German rivers and lakes is now quite clean and it is getting cleaner all the time. This is due to a ten point program that came into effect in the early 1980s. At that time people were shocked to discover that seals were dying in large numbers along the North Sea coast. Of course, all the pollution in Germany's rivers eventually ends up in the North and Baltic Seas, and the sea is also polluted with discharges from ships and oil rigs, such as oil and heavy metals.

"Since the early 1980s, all sewage plants have had to change their operations to remove more polluting substances, and all industrial waste water has to be cleaned before it is released into the general sewers. German water is now much cleaner, and the amount of pollution flowing into the sea has been reduced. Making further progress will depend on working with all the other countries that border the North Sea and the Baltic, but there are plans to remove all the main sources of pollution over the next 20 years."

◀ The water quality of the Chiemsee in Bavaria has improved dramatically since the 1970s due to better sewage treatment facilities and the use of phosphate-free washing products.

Waste and Waste Disposal

Living standards in Germany are very high. Large quantities of consumer goods are bought and used daily. Many goods are sold in too much packaging, creating waste. Goods that are no longer needed or wanted are thrown out and replaced by new ones.

For years, each household had just one gray garbage can for its waste. It was emptied once a week, and the garbage was taken to one of the many landfills or burned in an incinerator. Gradually, the cans became too small for all the garbage that people were throwing away, and the landfills were full. Waste disposal also had an effect on the environment: chemicals seeping out of the garbage polluted land and water, and burning waste in incinerators polluted the air.

▼ *Markets are popular in Germany. Not only are the products fresh, they are not wrapped in unnecessary plastic.*

Recycling and Re-use

People became aware that they were producing too much garbage. Not only was it damaging to the environment, it was also using up valuable resources, such as the wood pulp used in making paper and cardboard. A different approach to garbage was needed, and in the early 1990s, waste management became a new industry. The aim was to reduce the amount of waste produced and to conserve raw materials.

Now, every household has several garbage cans of different colors. Waste is separated and put into the appropriate container: blue is for paper, yellow is for plastic and metal, brown for biodegradable waste, and gray for all the garbage that cannot be recycled. Glass is taken to municipal bottle banks, where there are also special containers for old clothes and harmful chemicals. Bulky objects such as refrigerators are collected twice a year. A "waste calendar" informs people when each type of garbage is collected. Since the introduction of these measures, the volume of waste has decreased considerably.

▲ *Drink bottles and crates can be returned to the store when empty and filled again by the manufacturer. This helps to reduce waste.*

IN THEIR OWN WORDS

"I'm Michael and I'm 14 years old. We have had separate cans for different types of garbage for as long as I can remember. When friends from abroad visit us they smile at us because we are so serious about separating waste properly, but I think it is very important. It might take a little longer than throwing everything away into one can, but you soon get used to it.

"People here don't only separate garbage, we also try to reduce the amount of waste we produce. We don't get free plastic bags in the supermarkets here, for instance, so I always take my own bags when I go shopping."

6

The Changing Population

Immigration

There are about 7.6 million immigrants living in Germany. This means that nearly 9 percent of the population is of non-German origin. The immigrants come from all over the world, with the biggest group—over 2 million—coming from Turkey. The next largest groups are Yugoslavs, Italians, and Greeks. There are three main reasons why people have come to live in Germany: work, political asylum, and German ancestry.

◀ Food stores run by members of Germany's large Turkish community are a familiar sight in many towns and cities.

After World War II, West Germany received financial aid from the United States, and its economy recovered quite quickly. However, it did not have enough workers for its developing industries. People from other countries, such as Italy, Spain, Greece, Turkey, and Portugal, were invited to come to Germany to fill the gap.

The German constitution contains a clause allowing anybody who suffers persecution in his or her home country to seek political asylum in Germany. Between 1990 and 1993, over 1.2 million refugees entered Germany. At the same time, Germany was trying to deal with the migration of people

IN THEIR OWN WORDS

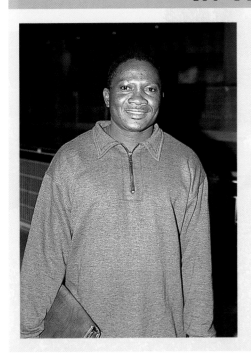

"My name is John Okoro and I am from Nigeria. I came to Germany as a political refugee three years ago. After a few months I met a German woman and we got married.

"I don't have any problems here in Germany, perhaps because I am married to a German. I do, however, know many immigrants who feel discriminated against, both at work and outside. They don't mix with Germans and live a totally separate life with their family and friends from their home country. Perhaps more effort should be made on both sides to get to know and understand each other better. Since 2000, immigrants have had the right to take German nationality if they have lived here for eight years; if they have children here, the children acquire German nationality at birth. Perhaps this change will help immigrants feel they belong here."

from eastern Germany to the west and with the costs of unification. Many Germans were out of work and experiencing a fall in their standard of living. There was a feeling that the country could not afford to take so many refugees. As a result, the law was changed. Refugees are now only granted asylum if Germany is the first safe country they enter after leaving their home country. Refugees who have passed through other countries must seek asylum there.

Many immigrants are of German origin. They come mainly from eastern Europe, where their families might have lived for a long time. Anybody with German blood is allowed to settle back in Germany. Many people have chosen to do so, even if they have never spoken the language or are unfamiliar with the German lifestyle.

▼ *These immigrants are learning German at one of the many schools that teaches German as a foreign language.*

Population Decline

The birth rate in Germany has been falling since the 1980s. Few families have more than two children, and an increasing number are choosing not to have children at all. The many methods of birth control available make it easy for people to decide whether to have children and, if so, how many. In a modern German family, this decision depends largely on whether the woman wishes to have a career or not.

Various studies carried out since the mid-1980s show that women who give up paid work to raise children want to go back to work after about seven years. This is roughly the time needed for one or two children to be old enough to go to a kindergarten or school. Women want to be financially independent, and they miss contact with other adults when they stay home as housewife and parent. Many women, of course, also need a paid job to help support the family.

Sources: UN Population Division; Geographical Digest; UNDP

▲ *Germany's population is expected to shrink over the next 50 years.*

◄ *Families with only one child are common.*

Tackling the Problem

A society needs young people to ensure progress. It also needs to have enough people working and paying insurance to fund adequate health and pension systems. Many laws and initiatives have been designed to make it easier for couples to

IN THEIR OWN WORDS

"My name is Sybille Kirschbaum and I live by myself. I have a good job as a civil servant and plenty of money for going out, shopping, and traveling. I don't have a partner or any children. This used to make me sad, but I am used to it now and I appreciate my independence and freedom. In the past, women were expected to get married and rely on their husbands to provide for them. Often they did not get the qualifications they needed to become financially independent. This has all changed now, and there are more and more single people living in Germany."

have children. For example, there is the right to a three-year parental leave, which can be split between the mother and father. During this leave, the parent's job is guaranteed and the parent receives a government allowance. Child benefits have also been increased.

◄ *The proportion of old people in the population is growing because fewer children are being born and people are living longer.*

7

Changes at Home

Changes in the Family

In the past, the roles within a family were quite clear: the man earned money for the family and the woman had children and looked after them at home. Depending on the social class and income of the family, the woman might also go out to work, but she was still responsible for the children.

◀ *This kindergarten in Stuttgart was built by Daimler-Chrysler for the children of its employees.*

Things are quite different now. Childcare facilities such as nursery schools and daycare centers mean that both parents can pursue a career if they choose. People can work from home, work part-time, or swap the traditional roles, with the father staying at home and the mother earning money for the family.

Whatever choice parents make, parenting and household tasks are generally shared today between the man and the woman. The stereotypical roles of the past have disappeared, and men are expected to cook, shop, clean, and take on all the tasks related to the upbringing of children. Children's relationships with their parents have changed too—studies show that many think of their mothers and fathers more as friends than as strict figures of authority.

IN THEIR OWN WORDS

"My name is Sabine Giese and I am a full-time mother. I gave up work when my son Felix was born ten years ago. It is normal for women in Germany today to get a good education and to pursue a career so that they can be independent. Many women then find it difficult to give up their career when they have children, and a lot of them choose to carry on working. I have always thought, however, that it is better for children to have a parent at home to look after them."

Single Parents

The number of single parents increased by 23 percent between 1991 and 2001. This sharp increase is partly due to the high divorce rate—39 percent of marriages ended in divorce in 2001. It is also partly due to changed attitudes in society—divorce or having children without being married is no longer seen as shameful. Single parents are mostly worse off financially than couples, and they have to work hard to juggle work and family life.

► *The increased demand for childcare has created new jobs for women like this kindergarten worker.*

Education

Schools in Germany are under the control of the federal states and, therefore, differ slightly from state to state. It is compulsory to attend school full-time between the ages of 6 and 15, and at least part-time between 15 and 18.

Children attend primary school for four years. They then go to one of three different types of secondary school, according to their abilities and interests. Some schools, for example, are for more academic pupils, while others take pupils who are better at practical subjects. Pupils attend secondary school for five, six, or nine years, depending on the type of school. Once they have finished school, they might choose to do three years of vocational training or enter higher education—if they have obtained the appropriate graduate certificate.

Young people in Germany have to do nine months' military or community service. This is seen as a way of making a contribution to society. Most people choose to do their military or community service before going to college, or after they have finished their vocational training.

▲ *A large, modern secondary school in Hamburg.*

Changes

The school system has hardly changed over the years, but the attitude towards education has. Education is seen as the key to getting a good job with high wages. Young people today leave school later and with better qualifications than their parents and grandparents. About 30 percent of all graduates have taken examinations that entitle them to go on to college. Most other graduates are qualified to take up an apprenticeship. Very few leave school without any qualifications at all. If they do, there are now many opportunities to study later in life.

IN THEIR OWN WORDS

"I am Walter Boiger and I am the head of a large comprehensive school in Hamburg. My school is special for two reasons. Firstly, it is comprehensive, whereas most schools in Germany are not. Secondly, it is a school where children stay all day. In most schools children start at 8 A.M. and finish at lunchtime.

"I think all-day schools are better, as it gives the children the opportunity to spend time together doing activities outside of the curriculum. For example, some of our older students run our school cafeteria as a proper business. They are supervised by the teachers, but they are responsible for the preparation and selling of the food as well as the administration and accounts. It is a great success."

The curriculum has undergone some changes. In addition to the traditional strong emphasis on math and German, greater importance is given nowadays to information technology, science, economics, and foreign languages. These changes reflect the skills that German companies need in order to compete in the global economy.

▼ Students enjoying their morning break.

Leisure Time

In spite of the general image of Germans as hard-working, their annual working hours are among the lowest in the industrialized world. The statutory maximum working time is 37.5 hours a week. On average, workers get 30 days of annual vacation plus several additional holidays for religious and national festivals.

What do Germans do with all their free time? They make the most of the escape from the daily routine. The most popular leisure activity is traveling. Germans of all ages travel whenever they can and wherever they can—not only within Germany and Europe but also to the farthest corners of the earth. Among young people the most popular leisure activities are sports, watching television, and spending time with friends.

Fifty percent of all Germans are members of at least one club, where they might spend an evening or two a week. There are clubs for virtually any interest, but the most popular ones are sports clubs, choirs, and orchestras. Classes where people can learn new skills, such as language or computer skills, are very popular, and so are classes teaching yoga or meditation, which help improve people's well-being.

▲ *In-line skating is a fun way to make the most of a sunny evening.*

IN THEIR OWN WORDS

"My name is Tom Attinger and I work as an engineer for a big company. I often have to work ten or eleven hours a day, and there is always a lot of pressure.

"In my free time, when I don't have to do any jobs in the house, I play music or listen to it, watch television, and spend time with my family and friends. I spend a lot of my free time playing sports, too. My doctor told me a few years ago that I was overweight and not very healthy. Now I go jogging four times a week, and I also ride up to 30 miles (50 km) on my bicycle twice a week. On Saturdays I play tennis at my local tennis club, and I try to ski as often as I can during the winter. I do feel much better now—better than I ever have before."

Festivals

Germans like celebrating, whether it is a family occasion such as a birthday or wedding, or an annual festival such as Christmas, Easter, or Carnival. Carnival celebrations take place in early spring, just before the Christian season of Lent. Carnival is especially important in areas where many people are Roman Catholics, such as southern Germany, and in the Rhineland, around Cologne. Parades are held in many cities, and people dress up in colorful costumes. The best-known festival is the Munich beer festival, which takes place in October each year and attracts many visitors. Christmas fairs and wine festivals are also very popular events.

▲ *The traditional beer festival is still very popular. This one is being celebrated at Rosenheim, near Munich.*

▼ *These women are dressed in traditional costume for a summer festival in Gluckstadt, near Hamburg.*

Healthy Living

Many Germans try to follow a healthy lifestyle and eat a good diet. There are a great many pharmacies and health food stores, and various magazines give advice on health. Spas and saunas have been popular for a long time, and more and more people now go to health clubs in their quest for a long and healthy life.

The Healthcare System

Everybody in Germany has health insurance. People who work share the cost of their health insurance with their employers. The government covers the costs for people who are not working. Health insurance pays for visits to the doctor and dentist, for hospital stays and rehabilitation programs, for prescriptions, and for benefits if a person is sick and unable to work.

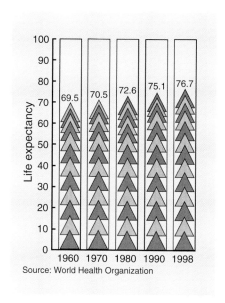

Source: World Health Organization

▲ *Germany's excellent healthcare system has contributed to the increase in life expectancy since 1960.*

◀ *Visiting spas—considered to be both healthy and relaxing—is a popular pastime.*

IN THEIR OWN WORDS

"My name is Herbert Kraus and I have been a pharmacist for 30 years. In the past, people came to me with prescriptions from their doctors. Most of the medicines I dispensed were to cure acute illnesses.

"Today, things are quite different. Doctors are not allowed to prescribe medication as much as they did before, and people are a lot more interested in trying to prevent illnesses. Now I find that people—especially those aged over 40—are buying vitamins, natural products to reduce their cholesterol level, and any other health product that might help to keep them feeling young and fit. I can also check people's blood pressure and measure their sugar and cholesterol levels. This is a really popular service now."

Germany's healthcare system is very good, but many people have taken advantage of it over the years. Perhaps they visited the doctor with minor problems that could easily have been treated at home, or they went to an expensive specialist without first checking whether their doctor could treat them. Improvements in drugs, equipment, and medical techniques caused the cost of healthcare to rocket.

Various measures to save money have now been introduced. The aim is to reduce unnecessary spending by doctors and patients without affecting the quality of healthcare. Doctors now have to prescribe the cheapest of the best available medication and patients have to pay for some preventative medical tests and special dental treatment.

▲ Health food and organic food stores are attracting more and more customers.

Food

Modern lifestyles and multicultural influences have changed the diet and eating habits of most Germans. Virtually any type of food is available. When, where, and what people eat have become very individual; it is nearly impossible to talk about typical German food and eating habits today. Young people enjoy pizza, spaghetti, or fast food such as burgers, washed down with soda, and they like to eat whenever they feel hungry. Older people might prefer a more traditional meal of meat, potatoes, and other vegetables, either eaten at lunchtime or in the evening after work.

▲ *A variety of German and foreign specialties being prepared for a summer street festival in Stuttgart.*

IN THEIR OWN WORDS

"I'm Helen and I'm 13. My friends and I love takeout food, but at home we have healthy food like pasta and vegetables. My mother, my sister, and I usually eat a hot meal at lunchtime at home. My father eats in the staff restaurant at work. In the evening we just have bread, salad, and meat or cheese.

"Neither of my parents likes cooking very much, so it's always very nice to have a meal at my grandmother's. She is a very good cook and she makes lovely roast dinners and a wonderful potato salad. Mmm!"

Although eating habits have changed—because more mothers now go out to work, for example—many German families try to eat together as often as possible. The family meal could be breakfast, brunch, lunch, coffee and cake in the afternoon, or dinner. Eating out does not have to be expensive, so it is also quite common for families to go to cafés or restaurants.

Traditional foods in Germany vary considerably from region to region, but different types of bread, beer, sausages, and sliced cold meats are popular all over the country. Cakes and gateaux are also eaten everywhere, not every day, but often for special occasions. Everybody—young and old—now includes foreign foods in their diet, the most popular being Italian. There are supermarkets, but many Germans buy their food in specialty stores or go to the market to get fresh and often locally produced food.

▼ *These men sell döner kebabs, one of the most popular foreign foods in Germany today.*

8

Changes at Work

Changing Industries

Germany's economy is based on industry, and since World War II, it has developed into one of the major industrial countries of the world. In the past, heavy industries such as coal-mining, iron and steel production, and shipbuilding were important. These industries have been in decline since the 1970s, partly as a result of increased competition from industries in other parts of the world.

Manufacturing

The principal industries in Germany today manufacture cars, machinery, and chemical and electro-technical products. Germany exports a lot of its products, so the names of companies such as Daimler-Chrysler and Volkswagen, which make cars, Siemens, which makes electro-technical products,

▲ A ship being built at a shipyard in Hamburg. Shipbuilding was once a major industry in the north, but now faces a constant struggle to survive.

and Bayer, which makes chemical and pharmaceutical products, are known worldwide. Germany is, after Japan, the biggest car exporter in the world. In 1998, its total GNP per capita was $26,570.

For several decades after World War II, German workers had job security, good wages, and good working conditions. But as firms introduced new technology, fewer workers were needed and jobs were lost. In the 1990s, an economic slow-down led firms to reduce their workforce in Germany. Many transferred their production to countries in eastern Europe and Asia, where wages and other costs are lower. German workers are getting used to less job security and higher unemployment.

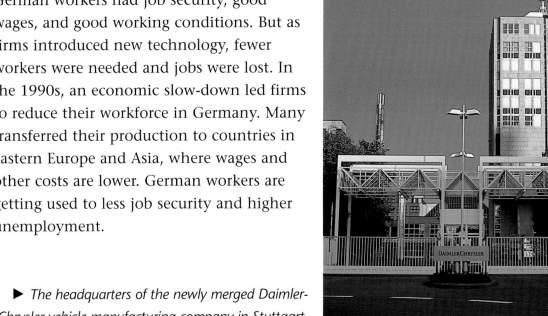

▶ The headquarters of the newly merged Daimler-Chrysler vehicle manufacturing company in Stuttgart.

IN THEIR OWN WORDS

"My name is Astrid Hobracht. I am an engineer and I work for LAUBAG, a company that mines lignite, in Cottbus. Before unification, Cottbus was in East Germany. Eighty-five percent of East Germany's energy came from lignite, but it caused terrible damage to the environment. So, after unification, lignite mining was severely reduced. Our company has only 4 of the 17 mines it used to operate left.

"We have introduced modern technology in our mines and power plants. The changes meant reducing the number of workers because machines can do a lot of the work, but we are efficient enough now to compete with other energy suppliers in electricity generation."

Competing for Business

Exports are important to the German economy, but competition from abroad is increasing. If customers can get better or cheaper goods and services elsewhere, German companies will lose business.

To maintain their competitive position, businesses in Germany have to control the amount of money they spend on pay and other benefits for their workers. German workers must now adapt to more flexible working arrangements. This might mean that they work for many different employers on short-term contracts, instead of staying with one employer throughout their working life. They might not do the same type of job for their whole life either. Training is important, to make sure that workers have the right skills for the jobs available.

At the same time, Germany needs to reduce its high level of unemployment, which has been rising steadily since the 1970s. To do this, it needs to encourage businesses to invest in the country so that more new jobs are created than traditional jobs are lost.

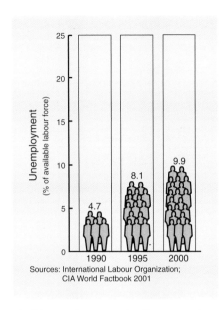

▲ *Unemployment in Germany has doubled since the early 1990s.*

The Euro

Germany adopted the euro as its currency in 2002. It took very little time for ordinary Germans to get used to the new currency, and business people were pleased with the change. Over 50 percent of Germany's trade takes place with other countries in the European Union, and when companies had to use different national currencies

▶ *This is Autostadt—a kind of theme park run by Volkswagen that is based around cars. Even long-established industries such as the car industry are having to find new ways to get people interested in their products.*

◀ *Industrial parks where small-scale industries are located have sprung up everywhere. These provide jobs, especially in some of the more deprived areas in the east.*

to buy and sell goods, the process took longer and created extra costs. Now Germany shares the same currency with 12 other countries in the EU, and trade with them has become easier.

IN THEIR OWN WORDS

"My name is Henning Flaig. I am 27 years old and I work for the Deutsche Bank in Stuttgart. The Deutsche Bank is one of the three largest banks in the world and has offices in 147 countries. The bank realized some time ago that a business could only be successful if it built up a worldwide network.

"I think that adopting the euro is good for the economy both in Germany and in Europe. It will lead to greater economic stability, and when there are problems with the economy in the United States, it should not affect us as much as it used to. I am quite optimistic as far as Germany's economic future is concerned."

Young Entrepreneurs

Young entrepreneurs are aged between 20 and 40 and are mainly found heading small and medium-sized enterprises (SMEs), which are firms with up to 500 employees. SMEs are of particular importance in Germany as they produce about 45 percent of the total economic output and employ 20 million people, which is 67 percent of the working population. They also train 1.2 million apprentices, about 80 percent of the total number.

Young entrepreneurs receive special help from the government, because they are seen as a driving force for new industries with new markets. They are not only creating jobs but also securing Germany's economic success for the future.

◄ *The workplace of a web-designer—one of the jobs that is increasingly in demand.*

Service Jobs

As more and more industrial production is moved to countries with lower wages, the service sector is becoming a more important source of employment. Experts believe that Germany is lagging behind countries such as the United States and Britain in this area, but the service sector's share of the gross national product is rising steadily. More than 1.5 million new jobs have been created since 1989 in areas such as software development, web design, consulting, marketing, and customer service, as well as in education, leisure, health and nursing care, domestic help, and childcare.

IN THEIR OWN WORDS

"My name is Hilke Langer and I am the press officer for 'Marketing Stuttgart.' We are responsible for promoting Stuttgart as an attractive destination for business people and tourists.

"Stuttgart has 1.1 million visitors a year. A few years ago, the number was much lower, because there was far less to see and do here. Now people come for all sorts of reasons: they might be taking part in a conference or a trade fair, or they might have come for an event such as a musical, an exhibition, or a concert. The festivals, such as our beer festival and wine festivals, attract a lot of visitors. Some people simply come to shop, especially around Christmas when we have the Christmas Fair."

Tourism

Germany is not only an important industrial nation, it is also a country that attracts many tourists. In the year 2000, 18 million foreign visitors came to Germany, 2 million more than in 1999. The most popular region is Bavaria, but the North and Baltic Sea coasts, the mountains and lakes, and some cities and towns are all tourist attractions. Tourism is the second-largest employer in the service industry.

▼ *Rowboats ready to be rented out to tourists at the Titisee, a vacation resort near the Black Forest.*

The Effects of Unification

The unification of Germany brought about many changes. The nationalized industries in the former East Germany had to be sold to and run by private owners, instead of by the government. Many firms had to close down because their products were old-fashioned and cost too much to produce in comparison with goods produced in other countries. In firms that did keep going, new technology and production methods were introduced. This generally resulted in at least two-thirds of the workforce losing their jobs.

The result was that unemployment, which did not exist under the regime of the East German government, began to rise. In some places, up to 40 percent of the workforce were unemployed.

◄ *These houses have been left empty as unemployed people moved from eastern Germany to look for jobs in the west.*

Economic Recovery

New investment was needed to boost economic development in the former East Germany and to create jobs for the many people who were out of work. The government of the unified Germany wanted to encourage international companies and companies from the former West Germany to set up businesses in the east. Before this could happen, the polluted environment of East Germany had to be cleaned up. New transportation links and communication networks also had to be built.

IN THEIR OWN WORDS

"My name is Carsten Seidel. I am from near Leipzig in eastern Germany. Like so many others, I lost my job soon after unification and was offered a place on a government retraining plan. I qualified as an electrician, but there were too many electricians and not enough jobs. It got harder and harder to find work, and the wages got poorer and poorer.

"Three years ago I decided to look for a job in the west because it was just getting too difficult to support my family. I could not afford to move my whole family to the west, so every Monday morning I commute for five hours to work and then I travel back on Friday afternoon. My nephew will be joining me soon—he wants to do an apprenticeship but he can't get one in the east."

All of these measures cost a lot of money. Germans had to pay higher taxes and the government had to borrow money. The result is a much weaker German economy. Tough measures are now being taken to reduce government spending and thus reduce the amount of money the government has to borrow.

▼ *A job-seeker arrives at a job center, hoping to find suitable work.*

9

The Way Ahead

Germany faces many challenges, especially in the changing world of work, but it has plans to tackle them. Until 2010, the number of people available for work will continue to expand and unemployment will remain a problem. After 2010, this problem will be reversed as the falling birth rate will lead to fewer young people starting work. Germany may then be short of workers. This shortage may be partially made up if more women take paid jobs and people from other countries come to work in Germany.

◀ Young Germans know their working lives will be very different from those of their parents, but they are confident about the future.

There is already a shortage of workers in some areas, such as information technology, engineering, and healthcare. The government hopes to fill these positions by attracting skilled people from abroad and by promoting training at home.

As the population gets older, the financing of the social security system will become a problem. A relatively small workforce will have to fund the growing population of older people. People might have to retire later. A reduced state pension supported by individual private pensions is another solution.

IN THEIR OWN WORDS

"I am Matthes and I am 18 years old. I will leave school next year. Young people in Germany have to do either military service or social work in the community. I am going to do social work and then I will go to college.

"I am looking forward to the future. I hope to get good qualifications and a good job. My generation might not work regularly all the time, but that does not matter, as it will give us more free time to do other things. I definitely want to have a family, perhaps when I am about 30. I could imagine staying at home for a while as a full-time parent."

Most young people in Germany are adapting to the changes taking place in their country. They are concerned about unemployment, but most believe that they will find good jobs if they are qualified. They do not expect to have lifelong employment in a full-time job, but they like the idea of flexibility, constant learning, and the independence that being in charge of your own career brings. They don't have any major fears, and they expect to have a high standard of living. They believe that the future of their country is bright.

▶ *Frankfurt am Main—the financial capital of Germany and the headquarters of the European Central Bank, which will play a crucial role in the economic development of the EU.*

Glossary

Apprenticeship A training program in which young people spend 80 percent of their time being trained at work by their employer, and the rest of their time at college. They have to pass practical and theory tests to become qualified.

Child benefit A payment made by the government to parents to help with the cost of bringing up a child.

Communist Relating to a political system in which ownership of private property is abolished and all businesses are run by the state on behalf of the people.

Comprehensive school A school that admits children of all ability levels.

Constitution The laws that set out how a country is to be governed.

Consumer goods Goods used in the home, such as TVs, washing machines, or CD players.

Conurbation An area where several towns or cities have grown bigger and joined together.

Emissions Waste gases or fluids.

Entrepreneurs Businesspeople who are prepared to take risks and try new ideas to try to make money.

Exports Goods that are sold to other countries.

Fallow Left empty, without crops.

Federal states The 16 states that make up Germany. Each state has its own elected government and has some freedom to decide its own policies, although foreign policy and economic policy are decided by the national government.

Fodder crops Plants grown to provide food for animals.

Global warming The increase in temperatures around the world, which scientists believe is the result of pollution in the atmosphere.

GNP (Gross National Product) per capita GNP is the total value of all the goods and services a country produces in a year, including investments in the country by other nations. "Per capita" is Latin for "per person," so GNP per capita is the total value of the goods and services divided by the total population.

Groundwater Water held underground in the soil and certain types of rock.

Hydroelectric power Electricity generated from turbines that are turned by the force of falling water.

Immigrants People who leave their own country and come to live in another country.

Imports Goods that are bought from other countries.

Infrastructure The network of transportation links, power supplies, factories, and training facilities that a country needs in order for its economy to work well.

Kindergarten Nursery school.

Life expectancy The length of time people can expect to live.

Municipal Relating to a town or city.

Nationalized Owned by the government.

Opencast mining Mining carried out by digging big holes in the ground, instead of tunnelling below ground.

Organic farming Farming without the use of chemicals, such as artificial fertilizers, or products that make animals grow faster.

Pesticides Chemicals used to kill insects that attack crops.

Political asylum People who seek political asylum are asking for protection from the government of their home country, which is attacking them because of their political beliefs.

Productivity The quantity of goods produced per worker.

Refugees People who have left their home country because they fear their lives are in danger because of war, natural disaster, or their political or religious beliefs.

Social security system Payments made by the government to help people who are out of work, on low incomes, etc.

Subsidies Money given to help with the cost of producing goods or services.

Unification Joining together.

Vocational training Training to do a specific job, such as plumbing or carpentry.

Further Information

Books to Read
Fuller, Barbara. *Germany (Cultures of the World)*. Chicago, IL: Benchmark Books, 1995.

Hirst, Mike. *Germany (Food and Festivals)*. New York: Raintree-Steck Vaughn, 1999.

Kelly, Nigel. *The Fall of the Berlin Wall: The Cold War Ends*. Crystal Lake, IL: Heinemann Library, 2001.

Lane, Katheryn. *Germany: The Land (Land, Peoples, and Culture)*. New York: Crabtree Publishers, 2001.

Pollard, Michael. *The Rhine (Great Rivers)*. Chicago, IL: Benchmark Books, 1998.

Schulte-Peevers, Andrea, Andrew Bender, Angela Cullen, and A. Haywood. *Lonely Planet Germany, 3rd Edition.* Oakland, CA: Lonely Planet, 2002.

Stein, R. Conrad. *Berlin (Cities of the World)*. Danbury, CT: Children's Press, 1997.

Websites
http://www.german-embassy.org.uk
This website includes information about German politics and current affairs, with reports on issues such as the phasing out of nuclear power.

http://www.germany-tourism.de/
A very useful website with information about German history, the federal states, cultural events and Germany's place in the international community.

Useful Address
German Embassy
4645 Reservoir Road, NW
Washington, D.C. 20007

Index

Page numbers in **bold** refer to photographs, maps, or statistics panels.